Dual Arrange[ments]

FOR THE
5-String Banjo

Frailing/Clawhammer *and* **3-Finger Scruggs Style**

by

Dick Sheridan

To access audio, visit:
www.HalLeonard.com/MyLibrary

Enter Code
7343-7732-4982-5047

Banjos on Back Cover:

LEFT: USA Custom Shop Recording King Top Tension Banjo Designed by **Greg Rich**
RIGHT: Recording King Ultra Deluxe Openback Banjo Designed by **Greg Rich**

Design & Typography by Roy "Rick" Dains
FalconMarketingMedia@gmail.com

ISBN 978-1-57424-334-5

Copyright ©2016 CENTERSTREAM Publishing, LLC
P. O. Box 17878 - Anaheim Hills, CA 92817
email: centerstream@aol.com • web: centerstream-usa.com

CONTENTS / SONG LISTING

THE AUTHOR REFLECTS

I've always felt that the 5-string banjo is something of a curiosity item. That 5th string drone is a puzzle, and it certainly has its harmonic limitations. My introduction to the instrument goes back to late grade school or early high school days when I spent a few days on Long Island in a primitive un-electrified cottage near the ocean that belonged to an octogenarian long retired from the Tiffany studios as a stained glass artisan. I discovered a 5-string banjo in the cottage and was fascinated by its odd configuration and unfamiliar tuning. I had already learned to play folk-style guitar and the ukulele, but this was something totally different. I asked my elderly host to play it for me, and with humorous eyes he strummed a basic chordal accompaniment and sang his version of a Harry Lauder song "My brother Jock's a baker and gets up each morn at three ..." For the duration of my stay I couldn't put the banjo down and unsuccessfully tried to make much sense out of it.

A number of years later while in college I began playing banjo with a campus Dixieland jazz band. I had been recruited because I could play a ukulele and a mandolin-banjo was found for me, reduced to four strings, and tuned like a uke. But the urge to find and play a real 4-string banjo led a classmate and me to prowl the music stores and hock shops of New York City in hopes of finding something suitable. Our search proved unproductive, just usually low-grade unclaimed instruments in moldy, musty-smelling cases pulled down from high shelves where they has been long forgotten.

But we did unearth something unexpected – several 5-string banjos in various states of disrepair. The instrument wasn't popular then and we definitely considered it to be an oddity. The only one I had ever seen before was the one from childhood days in the cottage on its sandy surrounds of Long Island, and that was probably ten years earlier.

Following the failed 4-string banjo search up and down the pawn shops of Eighth Avenue and the Bowery of lower Manhattan, I no more thought about 5-string banjos until several years after college when a visit to a musical museum in Deansboro, in upstate New York, revealed one hanging on the wall. Intrigued by it and with a renewed sense of curiosity I asked the museum's curator if he would sell it to me. He replied that it was not much of an instrument but gave me the name of a former vaudevillian in the area who might have a good one to sell. I made contact and arranged a meeting, the memory of which is vivid: as I started to climb the stairs to his apartment I was surrounded by the sound of a banjo echoing down the long flight; apparently the vaudevillian had been waiting for me, sitting at the top of the stairs, and with a sense of the theatrical had prepared a welcoming serenade.

Vaudevillian, Chet Pickard (aka Ted Shawnee), and accompanist friend, Barbara. It was from him that I obtained my first 5-string banjo, one that had belonged to concert performer, Alexander Magee.

Paul Cadwell - classical banjoist and familiar figure at folk music festivals and concerts. Frequent radio performer in the 1930s, soloed with the NBC Symphony, guest appearance on Pete Seeger's early TV show Rainbow Quest.

His name was Chet Pickard (stage name Ted Shawnee). We became friends and I purchased a 5-string banjo from him, an instrument with a large 12-inch head, that had belonged to a virtuoso concert hall performer, one Alexander Magee. (See Note at the end of this section.) My versatile new friend was not only a banjoist but a flyer who also claimed to have been a private pilot for bandleader Guy Lombardo. He arranged a special introduction for me to meet Paul Cadwell, a fascinating banjoist then vacationing in the Adirondacks. Tall and stately, then in his 70s, a graduate of Princeton and Harvard Law School, Cadwell played an intricate finger-style of banjo called classical, something I had never heard before. Highly accomplished, his playing was so much different from bluegrass that was just emerging in popularity, or the style of Dave Guard who played 5-string banjo with the folk group The Kingston Trio that topped the charts in the late 50s and early 60s. Despite his own virtuosity, Cadwell remarked about the high-speed playing of banjoist Roger Sprung, sometimes referred to as the NYC father of eastern urban bluegrass.

The purchase of the Magee banjo led to a spree of collecting vintage 5-string banjos so that at one point I had over 30 of them. As the banjo has surged in popularity and the demand for instruments increases, it's interesting to see new luthiers producing high-quality instruments, many elaborately ornate, that equal or exceed the craftsmanship of early makers.

Initially my 5-string banjo playing was limited to just strumming chords and picking out single melody notes. Gradually I became aware that the time value of single-note melodies could be stretched out by adding what are now referred to as "rolls" or which I sometimes call "patterns." This revelation was a major breakthrough in my playing and was the forerunner of the 3-finger Scruggs style songs in this collection.

Concurrent with this was the growing awareness of another style often called old-timey, frailing or clawhammer. There was a nearby music store whose proprietor played this style; whenever I stopped in the store I would ask for a demonstration and try to figure out what he was doing. Little by little the mystery cleared and a new world of playing enjoyment emerged.

Students often say they prefer this style because it allows them to play at a speed faster than what they are able to manage with 3-finger picking – and they don't have to wear finger picks.

My journey with the 5-string banjo has produced unexpected twists and turns leading to personal satisfaction, interesting experiences, and friendships I highly value. For the decades of years that I have taught, many students have become life-long friends, and for that I am ever grateful.

You are part of the 5-string banjo legacy. And whether you play with a group or strictly for your own amusement, the rewards are rich and enduring. The following songs will certainly enhance your enjoyment and add dimension to your repertoire. The convenience of having the same song presented in two styles side by side is not only fun but also introduces a valuable element of variety to your playing.

Note: For a rare recording of Alexander Magee playing "Southern Kaffe Klatch" in the classic 5-string banjo style, check out his name and the website: *The American Banjo Fraternity/Facebook*. A good photo is included. The banjo Magee is shown holding is not the one I obtained from Chet Pickard, but it does have the large 12-inch head like mine.

ROLLS AND PATTERNS

L = Lead note, numbers are string numbers,
T - Thumb, M = Middle Finger, IN = Index Finger

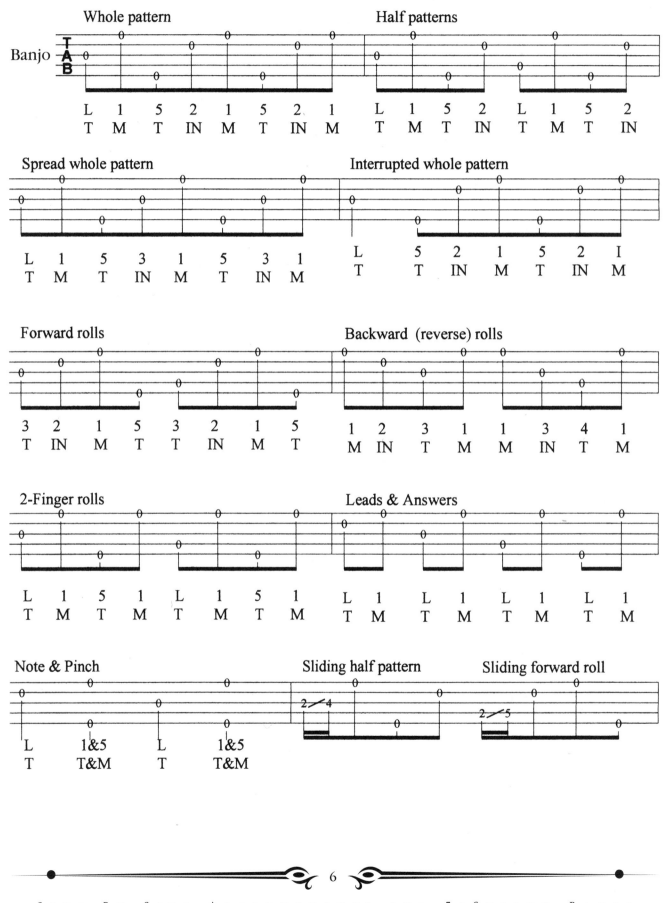

ROLLS AND PATTERNS

Hammer-On half patterns

Pull-Off half patterns

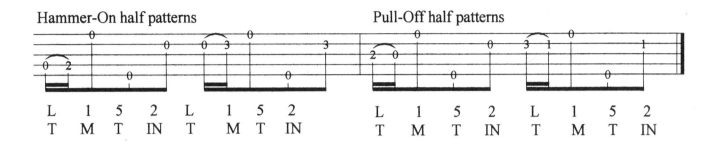

L	1	5	2	L	1	5	2
T	M	T	IN	T	M	T	IN

L	1	5	2	L	1	5	2
T	M	T	IN	T	M	T	IN

HAMMER-ON:

This is a 2-for-1 technique in which 2 notes are sounded but the string is only picked once. The first note is played by picking the string, the second note is sounded by a finger coming down hard on a higher fret without picking the string again. The sequence is always from a low fret to a higher one, or from an open string to a fret.

PULL-OFF:

Like the hammer-on, the pull-off sounds 2 notes, but only picks the string once. A fretted note is played and then by snapping it sideways to a lower fret on the same string (or to the open string), a second note is sounded. Pull-offs ad hammer-ons are indicated by a curved arc over two notes.

SLIDE:

The important note of a slide is the ending note. Keep pressure on the starting note and don't be too quick in releasing the ending note. It's not important where the slide begins but where it ends. Be careful not ot overshoot or undershoot the ending note, since this is usually a melody note. A slide is indicated by a diagonal line between two notes. Slides are usually from a low fret to a higher one, but ther order can be reversed.

LEAD & ANSWER:

This is a 2-note sequence, a melody or rhythm note ("lead") on an inside string followed ("answered") by the 1st string. The sequence can also be played in reverse with the lead note on the 1st string and answered by the 5th string.

BEAMS:

A beam is the heavy line connecting the bottom of note stems. Whole patterns have an 8-note beam. Interrupted whole patterns have a 6-note beam. Half patterns, forward & backward and 2-finger rolls have a 4-note beam. The lead and answer has a 2-note beam.

BRUSH:

All 5 strings are played together.

BILE 'EM CABBAGE DOWN
(3-FINGER STYLE)

G Tuning: gDGBD

TRADITIONAL

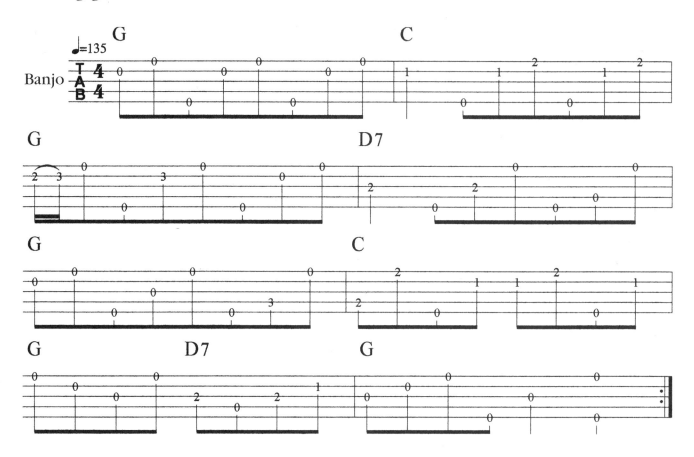

Bile 'em cabbage down, boys,
    Bake them biscuits brown,
The only song I ever could sing was
    "Bile 'Em Cabbage Down."

Raccoon up a cinnamon tree,
    Possum on the ground,
Possum says to the old raccoon,
    "Won't you throw some cinnamons down."

Went up to the mountain
    To give my horn a blow,
Thought I heard my true love say,
    "Yonder comes my beau."

Took my girl to the blacksmith shop
    To have her mouth made small,
She turned around a time or two
    And swallowed that shop and all.

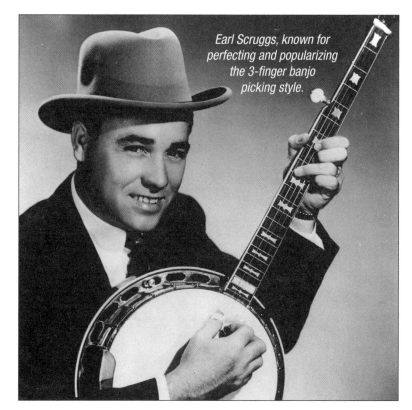

Earl Scruggs, known for perfecting and popularizing the 3-finger banjo picking style.

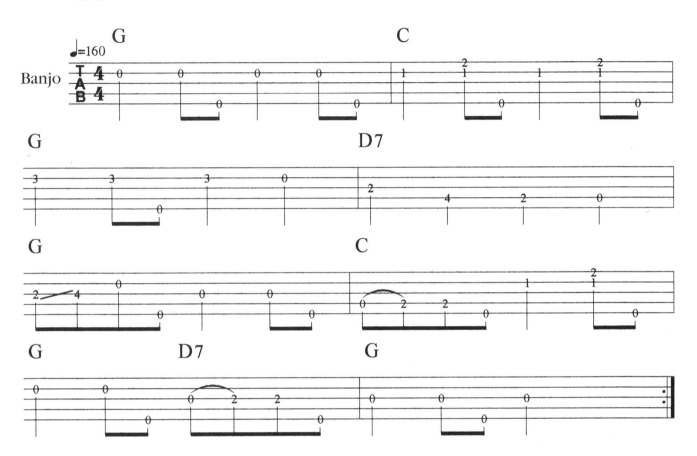

BILE 'EM CABBAGE DOWN
(FRAILING / CLAWHAMMER)

G Tuning: gDGBD

TRADITIONAL

Wade Ward, early master of the clawhammer style of banjo playing.

CLUCK OLD HEN
(3-FINGER STYLE)

G Tuning: gDGCD

TRADITIONAL

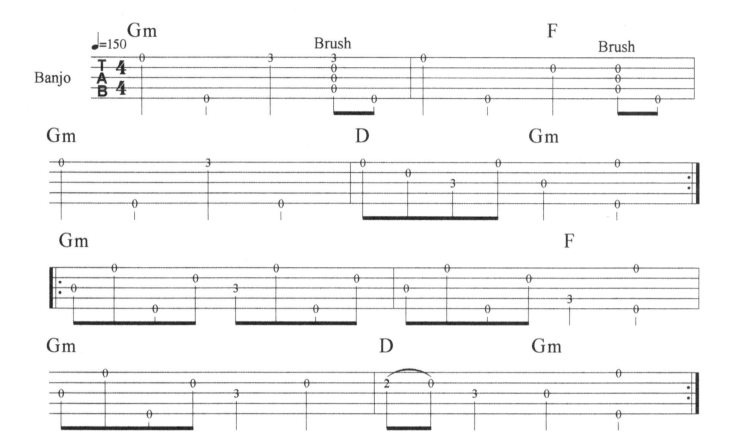

My old hen, she's a good old hen,
    She lays eggs for the railroad men.
Sometimes one, sometimes two,
    Sometimes enough for the whole dang crew.

Cluck old hen, cluck and call,
    You ain't laid an egg since way last fall.
Cluck old hen, cluck and sing,
    You ain't laid an egg since way last spring.

Pete Seeger - multi-instrumentalist, folk singer and social activist. He wrote the book, "How to Play the 5-String Banjo" which many famous players cite as their introduction to playing the instrument. He was a prolific songwriter, anti-war advocate and was even responsible for bringing Bob Dylan to the attention of Columbia Records.

CLUCK OLD HEN
(FRAILING / CLAWHAMMER)

G Tuning: gDGCD

CRIPPLE CREEK
(3-FINGER STYLE)

G Tuning: gDGBD

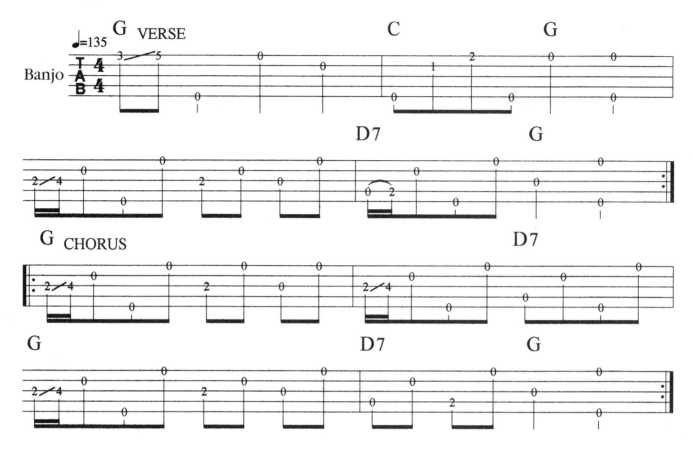

VERSE

Cripple Creek's wide and Cripple Creek's deep,
    I'll cross Cripple Creek 'fore I sleep.
Roll my britches up to my knees,
    I'll cross Cripple Creek when I please.

CHORUS

Goin' down to Cripple Creek,
    Goin' on a run,
Goin' down to Cripple Creek,
    Have a little fun.

Goin' down to Cripple Creek,
    Goin' in a whirl,
Goin' down to Cripple Creek
    See my girl.

Charlie Poole and the North Carolina Ramblers, circa 1925. Poole developed a unique three-fingered style due to a baseball accident that broke his thumb and left his hand in a permanent arch. The group had a string of hits from 1925 to 1930.

CRIPPLE CREEK
(FRAILING / CLAWHAMMER)

G Tuning: gDGBD

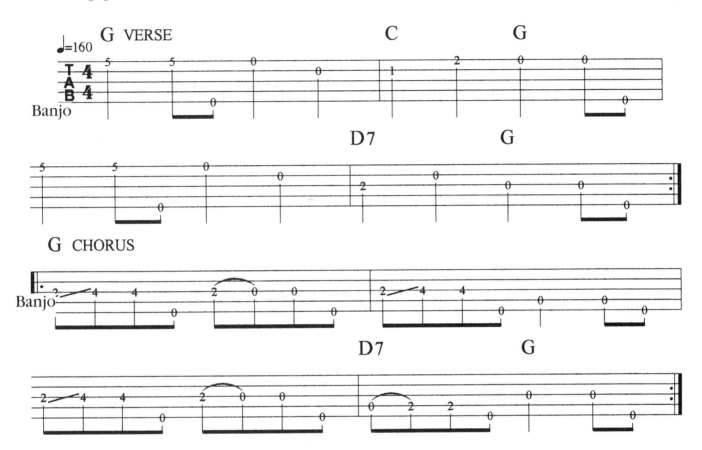

Ralph Stanley has been playing music professionally since 1946, both as a member of the Stanley Brothers and the Clinch Mountain Boys. He learned to play clawhammer banjo from his mother, and from that basis developed his own unique style.

The CHORUS of "Cripple Creek" is the same as the short song, "Cotton-Eye Joe." There are many variations but this CHORUS version is popular and as good as any.

COTTON-EYE JOE

1. Where do you come from,
   Where do you go,
   Where do you come from,
   Cotton-Eye Joe?

2. I come for to see you
   And I come for to sing,
   Come for to show you my
   Diamond ring.

3. Cotton-Eye Joe,
   Cotton-Eye Joe,
   Whatever made you
   Treat me so?

4. Took my gal
   Away from me,
   Took her down to
   Tennessee.

5. Hadn't it been for
   Cotton-Eye Joe,
   I'd a-been married a
   Long time ago.

CUMBERLAND GAP
(3-FINGER STYLE)

G Tuning: gDGBD

TRADITIONAL

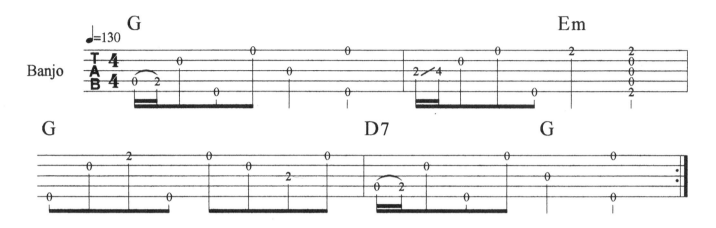

Banjo

Cumberland Gap's a fine old place,
    Three kinds of water to wash your face.

Me and my wife and my wife's pap,
    We all went down to Cumberland Gap.

Lay down, boys, take a little nap,
    Fourteen miles to Cumberland Gap.

The Cumberland Gap is a mountain pass where the three states of Kentucky, Tennessee and Virginia come together. It was a favored route for settlers on their westward migration.

Steve Martin, who became famous for his standup comedy in the 1970s, first picked up the banjo at the age of 17, and received some instruction from John McEuen of the Nitty Gritty Dirt Band. The banjo became a regular feature of his comedy routines. When Martin retired his standup act, he devoted himself to writing, producing and deeper study of the banjo. He has performed regularly with bluegrass group, The Steep Canyon Rangers.

CUMBERLAND GAP
(FRAILING / CLAWHAMMER)

G Tuning: gDGBD

TRADITIONAL

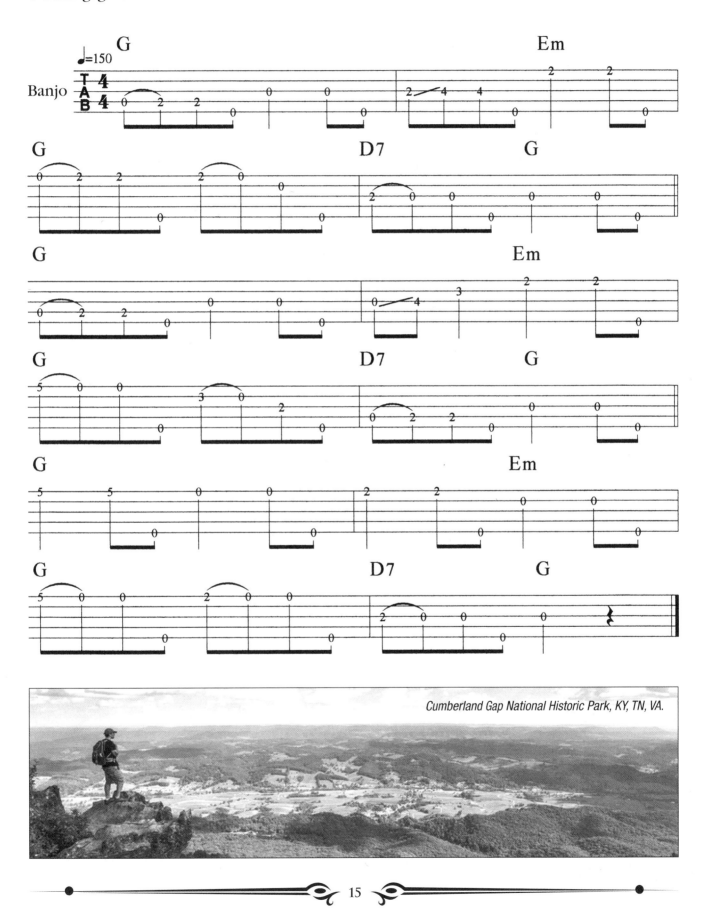

Cumberland Gap National Historic Park, KY, TN, VA.

SIDE BY SIDE ARRANGEMENTS FOR 5-STRING BANJO

Darlin' Corey
(3-FINGER STYLE)

G Tuning: gCGCD

TRADITIONAL

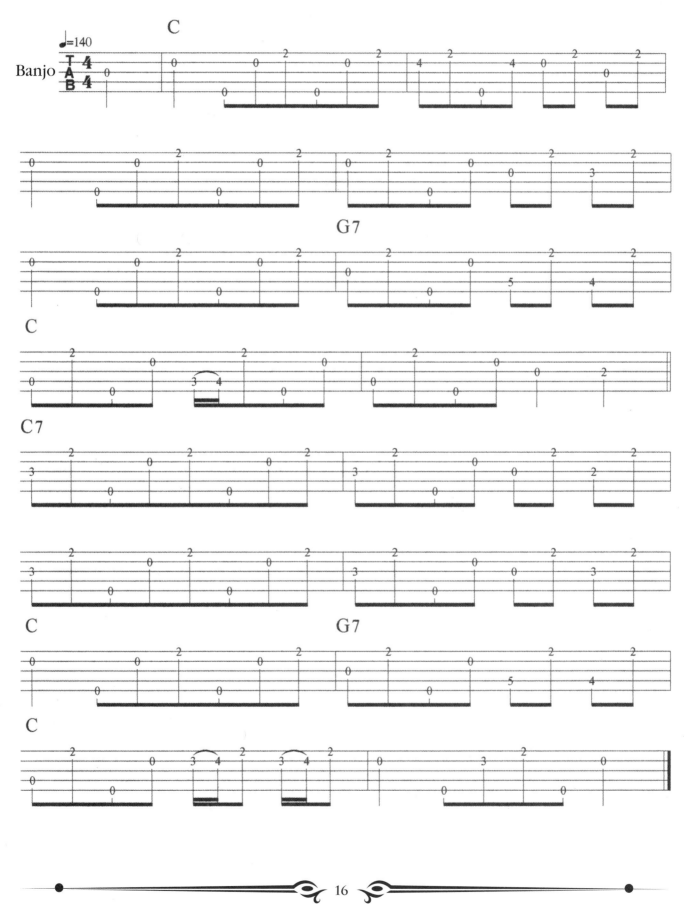

Darlin' Corey
(FRAILING / CLAWHAMMER)

G Tuning: gCGCD

TRADITIONAL

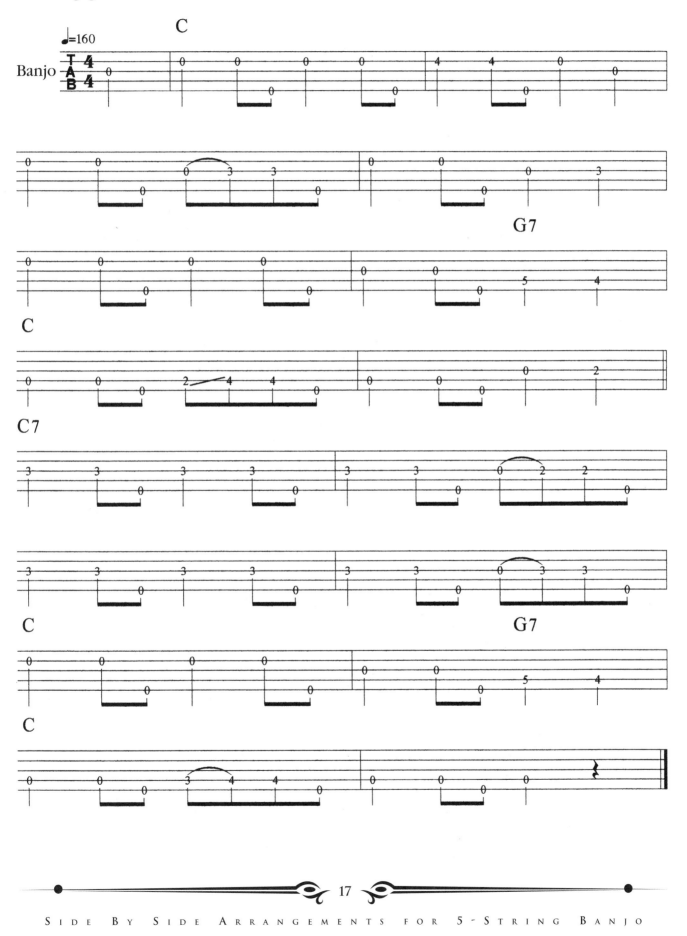

Distant Thunder
(3-FINGER STYLE)

G Tuning: gDGBD

DICK SHERIDAN

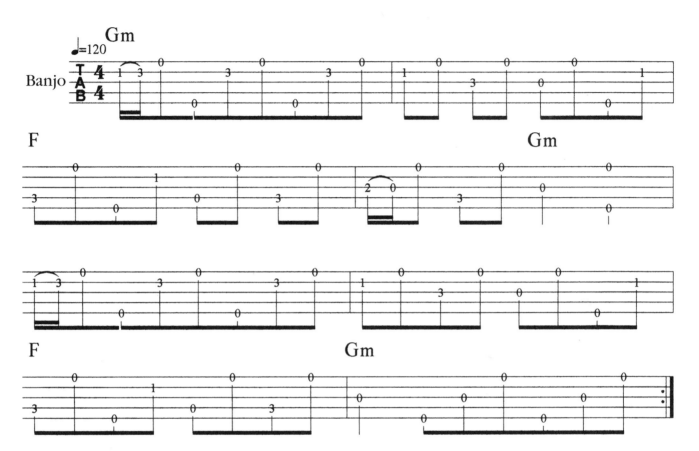

The sound of this song is modal, but instead of going to a modal tuning (gDGCD), hold down the 1st fret of the 2nd string which produces the C note of modal tuning. For a more "lonesome" sound, try substituting a G major chord for the G minor.

John Hartford was an American folk, country and bluegrass composer and musician known for his mastery of the fiddle and banjo. He was revered for his unique and unorthodox style of playing and is considered a co-founder of the Newgrass movement of the early 1970s. He wrote the classic, "Gentle On My Mind" which won four 1968 Grammy awards. He also won a Grammy for his work on the soundtrack for the Coen Brothers film, "Oh Brother, Where Art Thou?"

DISTANT THUNDER
(FRAILING / CLAWHAMMER)

G Tuning: gDGBD

DICK SHERIDAN

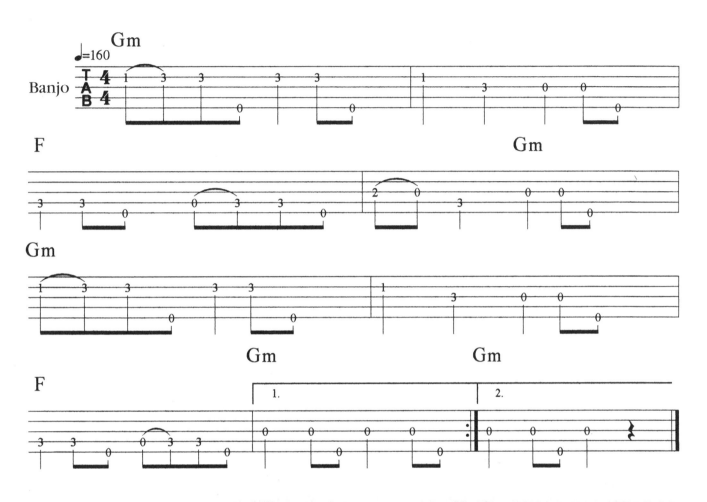

Bob Carlin is an "old-time" banjo player, specializing in the clawhammer style. He is also a musical historian, playing legacy instruments, including gourd banjos. He is also studying the African roots of the banjo. He toured for several years with John Hartford and is also a producer and the founder of CarTunes Recordings.

OLD BEN
(3-FINGER STYLE)

G Tuning: gDGBD

DICK SHERIDAN

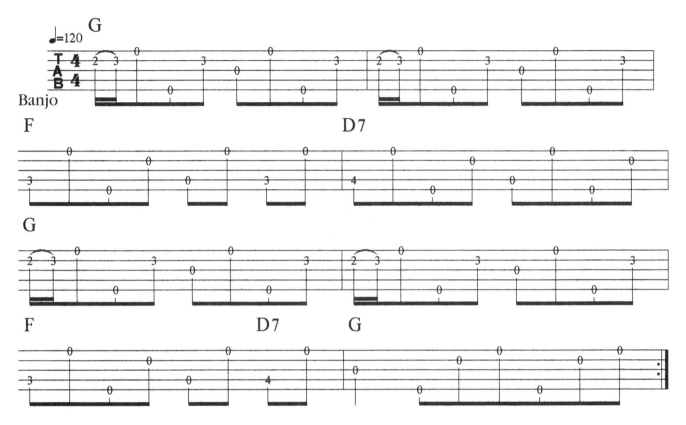

John McEuen - songwriter, producer and
session musician. McEuen is a highly
prized multi-instrumentalist, appearing
on countless recordings for top artists
from the 1970s to the present. He is also
a founding member of the 1970s country
folk rock group The Nitty Gritty Dirt Band.

OLD BEN

(F R A I L I N G / C L A W H A M M E R)

G Tuning: gDGBD

DICK SHERIDAN

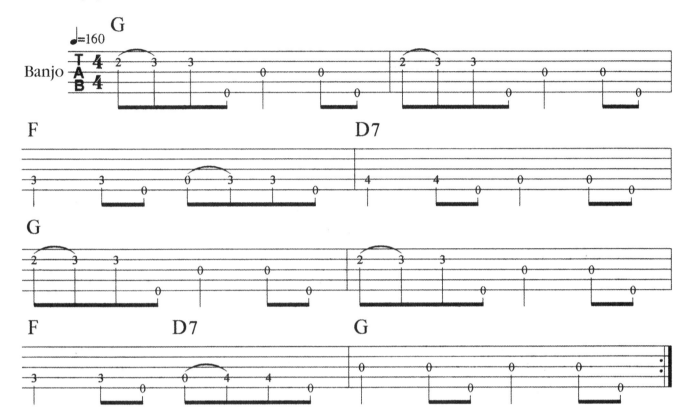

Leo McFurrée - Early master of "claw"hammer style banjo.

Old Ben lived above the stairs,
    Preacher tried but couldn't ever make him say his prayers.
He'd put up an awful fight,
    Never took a bath on Saturday night.

Dog barked, Bossy wagged her tail,
    Chicken chased a rooster around the pail,
Sow-ee! Brush away your tears,
    Pig snapped his fingers and wiggled his ears.

Banjo, fiddle and a bow,
    One plays high and the other plays low,
Sing-song, move it right along,
    Mind the music and you won't go wrong.

Old Ben, whiskers to his knees,
    Store-bought shoes and BVDs,
Corncob pipe hanging from his mouth,
    Packin' his bags and headin' down south.

OLD GROUNDHOG
(2-FINGER STYLE)

G Tuning: gDGBD TRADITIONAL

Try playing this style using just the thumb and index finger of the right hand.

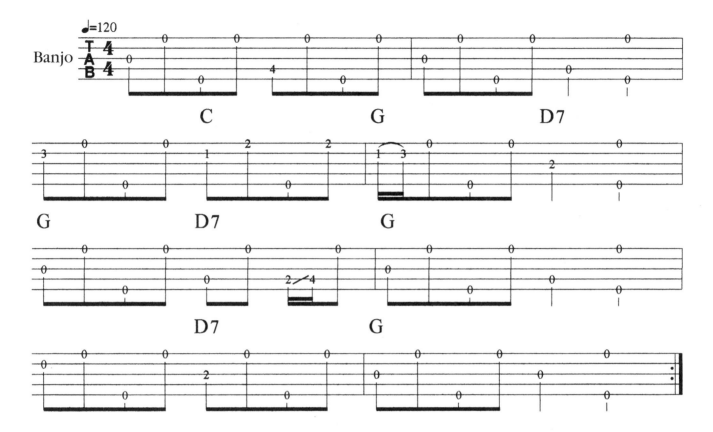

1. Whet up your knife and whistle up your dog,
        Whet up your knife and whistle up your dog,
    We're off to the woods to hunt groundhog,
        Old groundhog!

2. The meat'll do to eat and the hide'll do to wear,
        The meat'll do to eat and the hide'll do to wear,
    If that ain't groundhog, I declare,
        Old groundhog!

3. Up steps Sam with a 10-foot pole,
        Up steps Sam with a 10-foot pole,
    Gonna roust that groundhog outta his hole,
        Old groundhog!

4. Up steps Sally with a snigger and a grin,
        Up steps Sally with a snigger and a grin,
    Groundhog juice all over her chin,
        Old groundhog!

OLD GROUNDHOG
(FRAILING / CLAWHAMMER)

G Tuning: gDGBD

GROUNDHOG DAY: Tradition has it that if it's sunny on February 2nd and a groundhog sees his shadow, winter will last another six weeks. On Gobblers Knob in Punxsutawney, PA, a groundhog named Phil is annually roused from hibernation and used as a weather predictor. The custom was brought to this country by German immigrants who settled in central Pennsylvania and substituted a groundhog for the badger that was typically used in Europe.

Hobart Smith was a master of clawhammer style, whose career started with performing at minstrel and medicine shows with his sister in the early 1900s. His talent eventually brought him to the attention of Eleanor Roosevelt, who invited him to play at the White House. The 1960s folk revival brought him back into the spotlight.

OLD JOE CLARK
(3-FINGER STYLE)

G Tuning: gDGBD

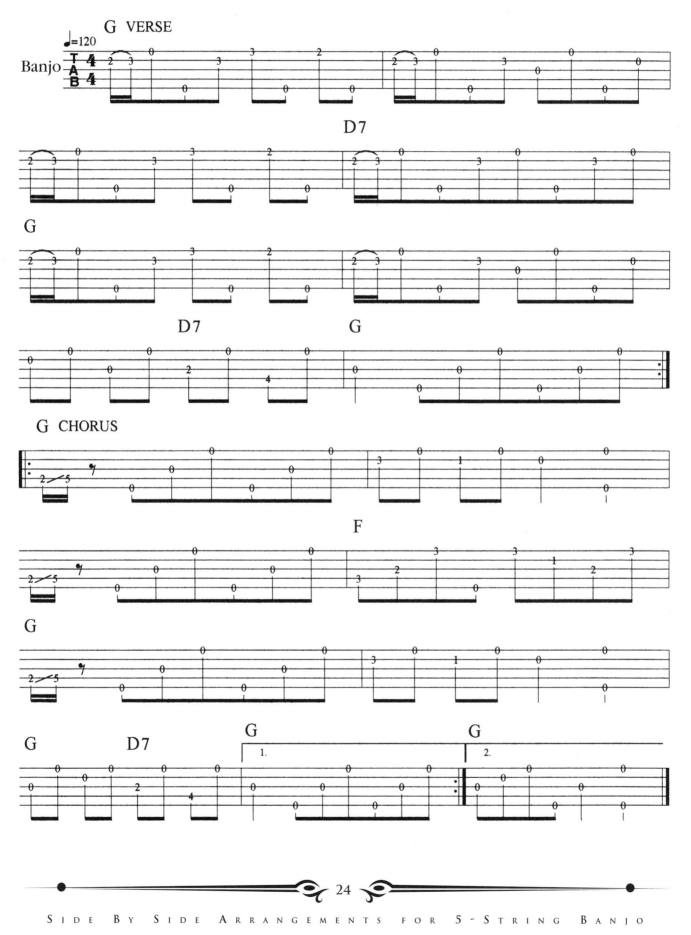

OLD JOE CLARK
(FRAILING / CLAWHAMMER)

G Tuning: gDGBD

TRADITIONAL

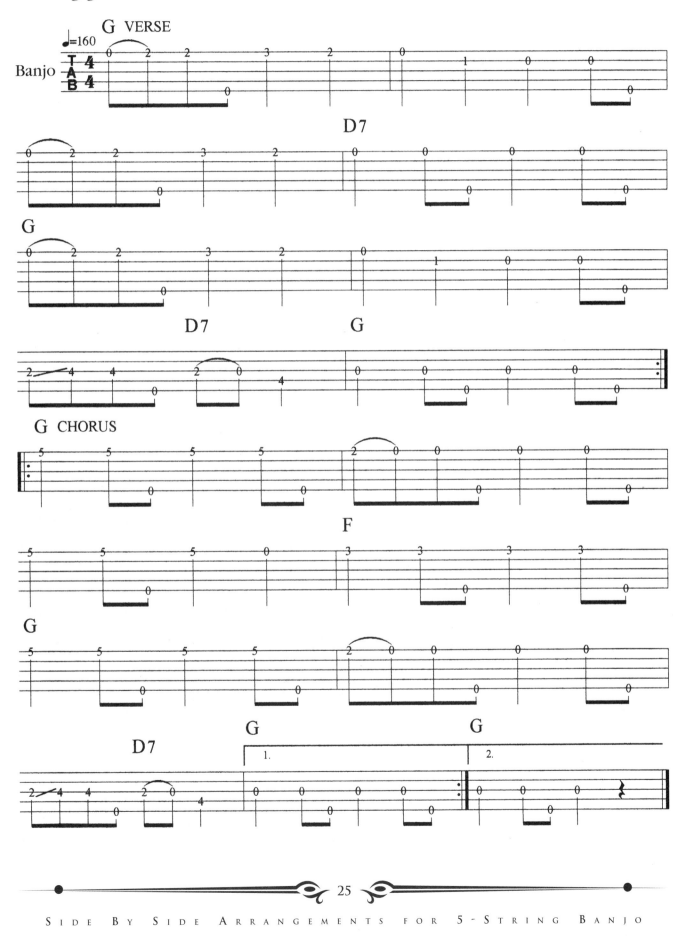

SIDE BY SIDE ARRANGEMENTS FOR 5-STRING BANJO

SHADY GROVE
(3-FINGER STYLE)

G Tuning: gDGCD

Banjo

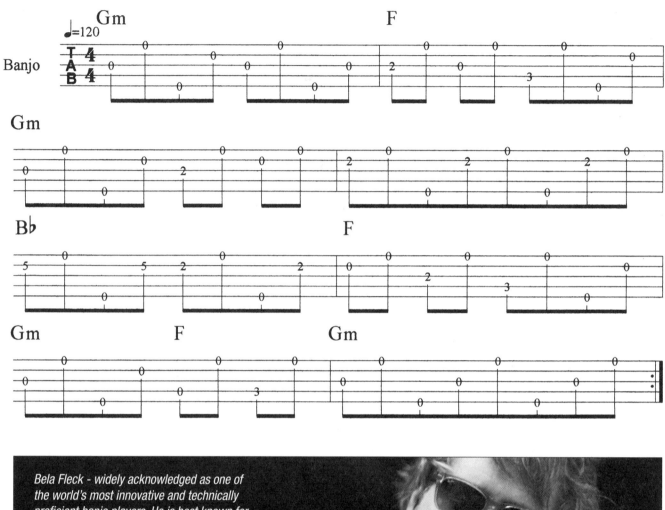

Bela Fleck - widely acknowledged as one of the world's most innovative and technically proficient banjo players. He is best known for his work with the bands New Grass Revival and Bela Fleck and the Flecktones.

SHADY GROVE
(FRAILING / CLAWHAMMER)

G Tuning: gDGCD

TRADITIONAL

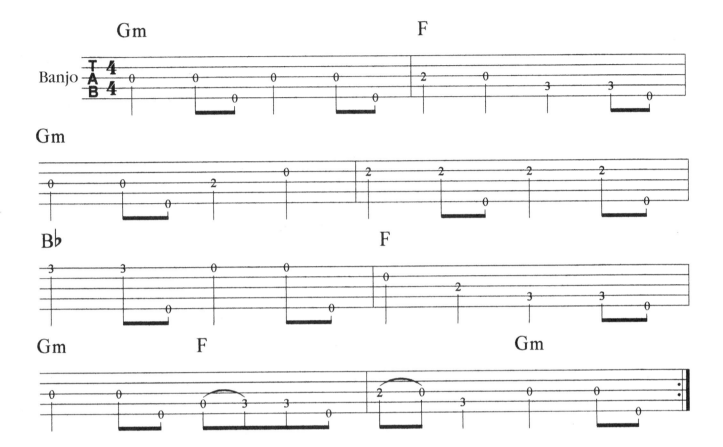

Shady Grove, my true love,
  Shady Grove, I know,
Shady Grove, my true love,
  We're bound for the Shady Grove.

Peaches in the summertime,
  Apples in the fall,
If I can't have the one I love
  I won't have none at all.

Shady Grove, my little love,
  Standing in the door,
Shoes and stockings in her hand,
  Bare feet on the floor.

Dick Kimmel is an "old-time" musician and biologist, specializing in clawhammer banjo, mandolin and guitar. He has been inducted into several music halls of fame and has been nominated as the Bluegrass Entertainer of the Year by the SPBGMA (the Society for the Preservation of the Bluegrass Music of America). He continues to write, record and perform both as a solo act and with his band, Dick Kimmel & Co.

Skip to my Lou
(2-FINGER STYLE)

G Tuning: gDGBD

TRADITIONAL

Try playing with just the thumb and index finger of the right hand.
To match the pitch of the frailing / clawhammer version, capo on the 5th fret.

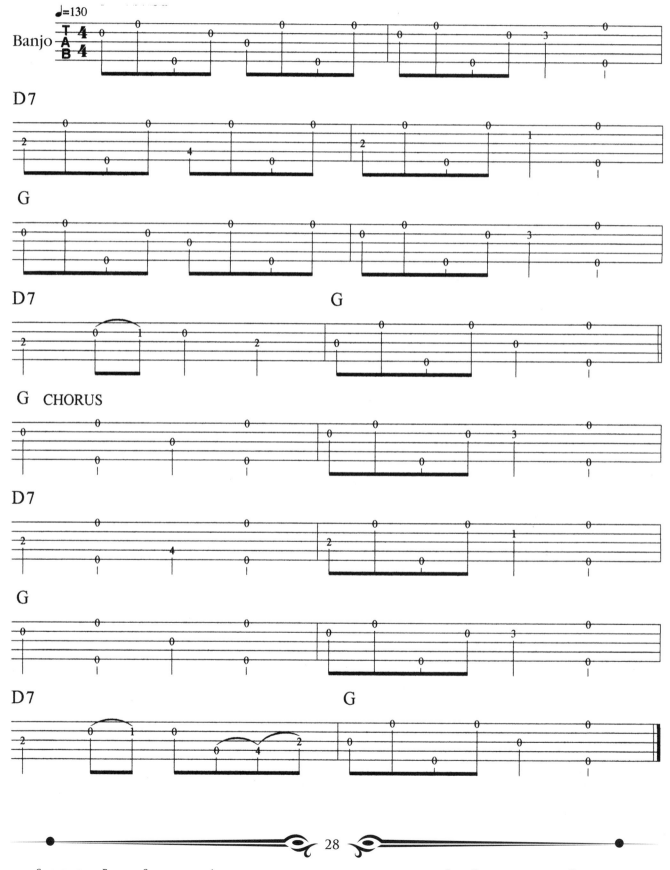

SKIP TO MY LOU
(FRAILING / CLAWHAMMER)

G Tuning: gCGBD

TRADITIONAL

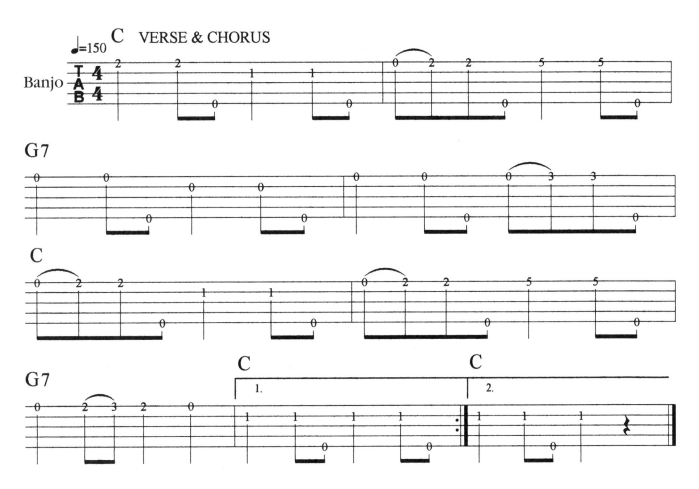

VERSES:

1. Flies in the buttermilk, shoo fly shoo,
       Flies in the buttermilk, shoo fly shoo,
    Flies in the buttermilk, shoo fly shoo,
       Skip to my Lou, my darling.
    CHORUS

2. I'll find another one prettier than you, (3X)
       Skip to my Lou, my darling.
    CHORUS

3. Little red wagon painted blue, (3X)
       Skip to my Lou, my darling.
    CHORUS

4. Dog ate my homework, what'll I do? (3X)
       Skip to my Lou, my darling.
    CHORUS

CHORUS:

Lou, Lou, Skip to my Lou,
   Lou, Lou, Skip to my Lou,
Lou, Lou, Skip to my Lou,
   Skip to my Lou, my darling.

SUGAR HILL
(3-FINGER STYLE)

G Tuning: gDGBD

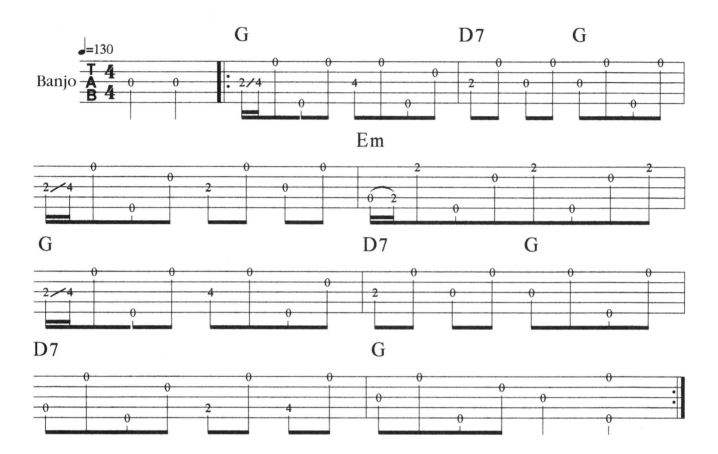

Tony Trischka - unquestionably one of the most consummate, innovative, and versatile banjo players on the current scene. Celebrated worldwide performer, prolific author of banjo books, online teacher, recording artists, PBS documentary producer, awarded the IBMA Banjo Player of the Year in 2007, named United States Artists Friends Fellow in 2012. Frequent radio and TV appearances with Earl Scruggs, Bela Fleck (who studied with Tony), Steve Martin and other prominent players.

SUGAR HILL

(FRAILING / CLAWHAMMER)

G Tuning: gDGBD

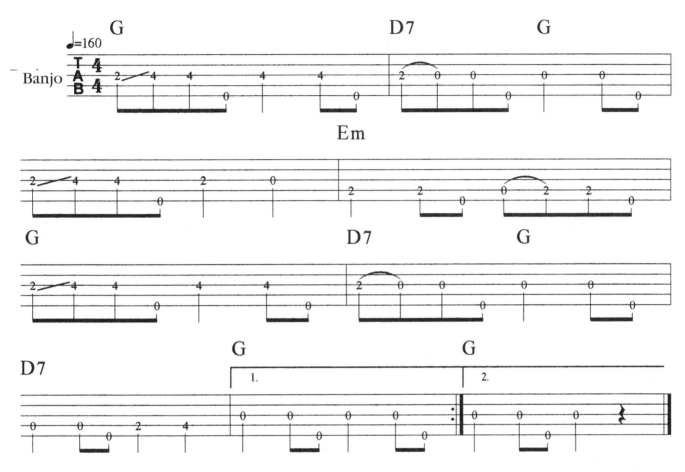

If you want to get your eye knocked out,
    If you want to get your fill,
If you want to get your head bashed in,
    Climb old Sugar Hill.

Ten cents in my pocket book,
    Change from a dollar bill,
If I had ten dollars more,
    I'd climb old Sugar Hill.

If I had no horse to ride,
    I'd be bound to walking,
Up and down old Sugar Hill,
    Give my girl a talking.

Roger Sprung - sprang from the 50s and 60s NYC Sunday afternoon folk gatherings of Washigton Square in Greenwich Village to become an urban interpreter of bluegrass in its more diverse and progressive forms. Influenced by Pete Seeger, Paul Cadwell, and Tom Paley of the New Lost City Ramblers, in turn influenced Eastern players like Tony Trischka and Bela Fleck.

TOBACCO JUICE
(3-FINGER STYLE)

G Tuning: gCGCD

DICK SHERIDAN

C7 Continue the C7 chord for the entire piece.

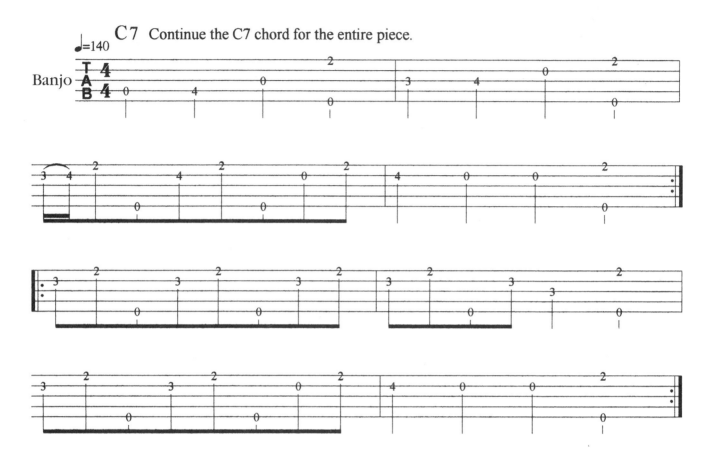

Todd Taylor is a Grammy-nominated bluegrass musician who has held the Guiness World Record for "Fastest Banjo Player." He is the first banjo player to appear on the Rock 'n' Roll Top 40, with his banjo rendition of "Free Bird." He gets a lot of recent attention on the internet for posting his banjo renditions of famous rock songs on YouTube.

TOBACCO JUICE
(FRAILING / CLAWHAMMER)

Double C Tuning: gCGCD

DICK SHERIDAN

C7 Continue the C7 chord for the entire piece.

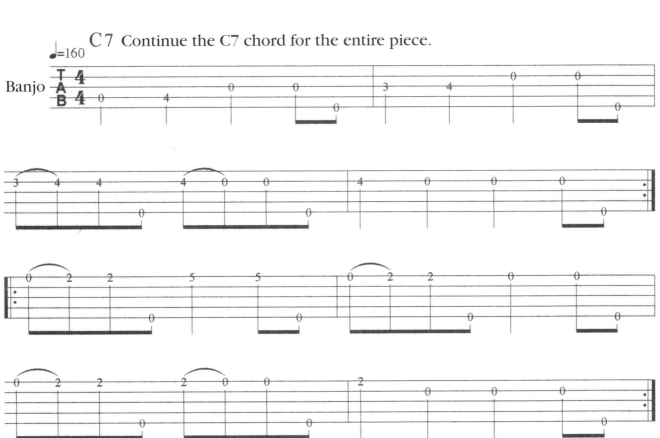

Nathan Bowles is an artistic standout in the latest wave of banjo players. He takes inspiration from traditional Appalachian folk music and imbibes it with elements of experimental music. This produces a self-aware exploration of the banjo's simplistic sounds and the complicated emotions they evoke. He describes his playing as "tranced-out solo clawhammer banjo."

TOM DOOLEY
(3-FINGER STYLE)

G Tuning: gDGBD

TRADITIONAL

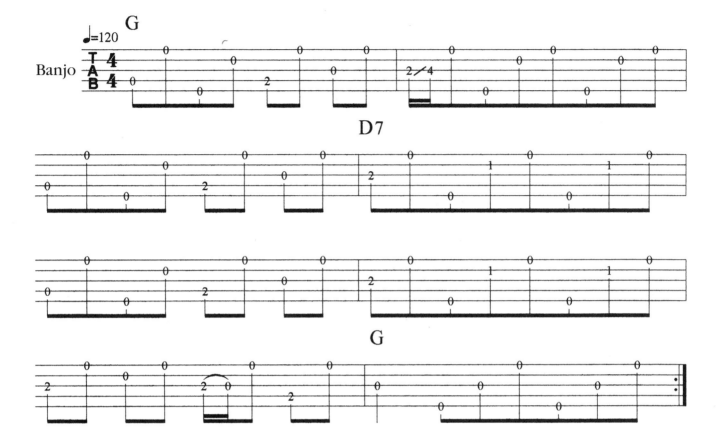

Hang down your head, Tom Dooley,
    Hang down your head and cry,
Hang down your head, Tom Dooley,
    Poor boy, you're bound to die.

Met her on the mountain,
    There I took her life,
Met her on the mountain,
    Stabbed her with my knife.

This time tomorrow,
    Reckon where I'd be,
If it hadn't been for Grayson
    I'd-a been in Tennessee.

This time tomorrow,
    Reckon where I'll be,
In some lonesome valley,
    Hanging from a white oak tree.

Jim Mills is a bluegrass player who spent a decade and a half playing for Ricky Skaggs and Kentucky Thunder. Since his departure from the band, he has concentrated on the acquisition and sales of pre-war Gibson banjos, of which he is an expert. Jim has won 6 Grammy awards, been the IBMA Banjo Player of the Year 6 times, and been awarded Instrumental Album of the Year by the IBMA for one of his solo albums.

TOM DOOLEY

(FRAILING / CLAWHAMMER)

G Tuning: gDGBD

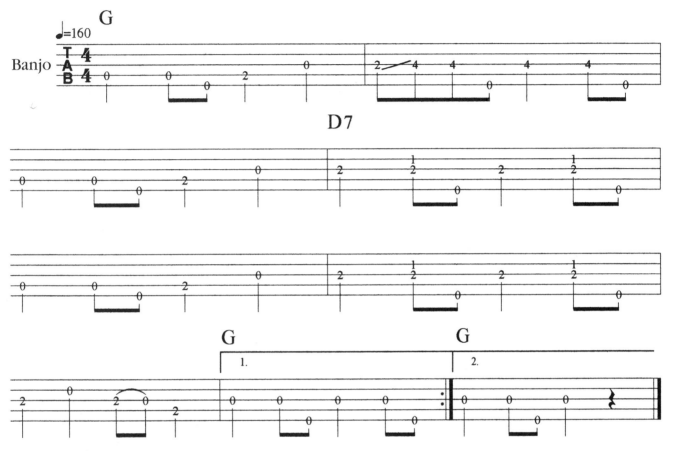

With a steady climb on the charts at the end of 1958, "Tom Dooley" by the folk group The Kingston Trio stayed in the top 10 for 12 weeks hitting the #1 spot in mid-November of '58. The song is often credited as being the influence for the boom in folk music of the 1960s.

Mike Seeger - acclaimed folklorist, singer, and accomplished multi-instrumentalist of traditional folk instruments. A dominant force in the folk revival of the 1960s, numerous recordings both as soloist and with the iconic group New Lost City Ramblers of which he was co-founder. Brother of folk singer Peggy Seeger (wife of British folk performer Ewan MacColl) and half-brother of Pete Seeger.

WHEN YOU AND I WERE YOUNG, MAGGIE

(3-FINGER STYLE)

G Tuning: gDGBD

TRADITIONAL

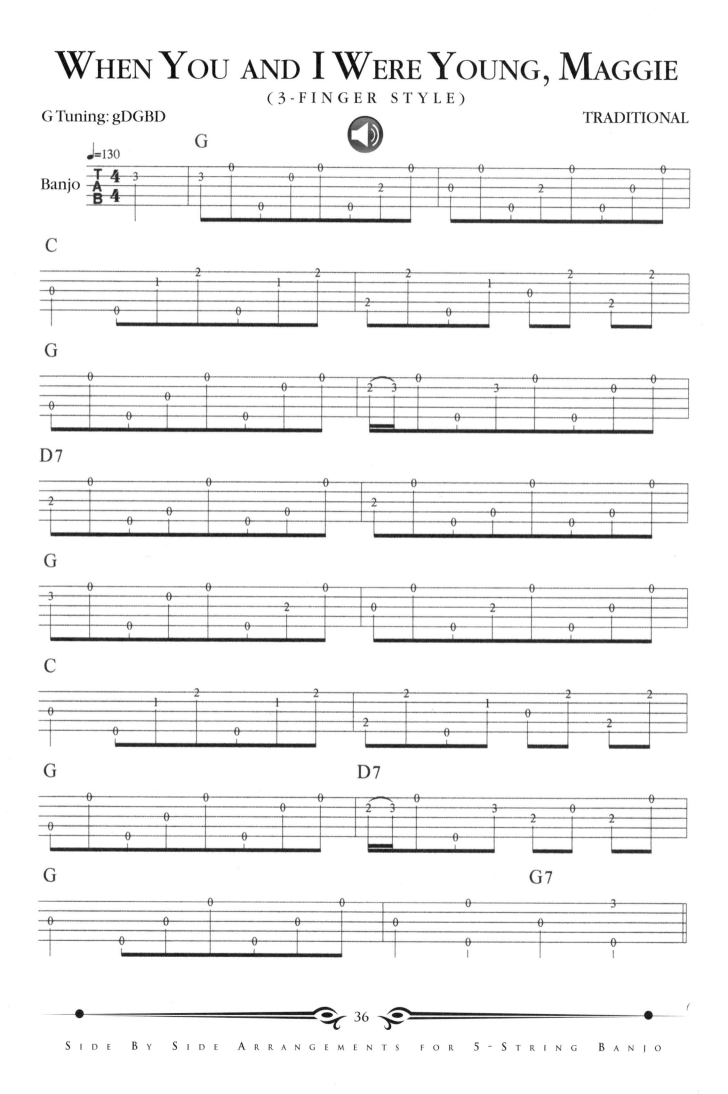

WHEN YOU AND I WERE YOUNG, MAGGIE
(3-FINGER STYLE)

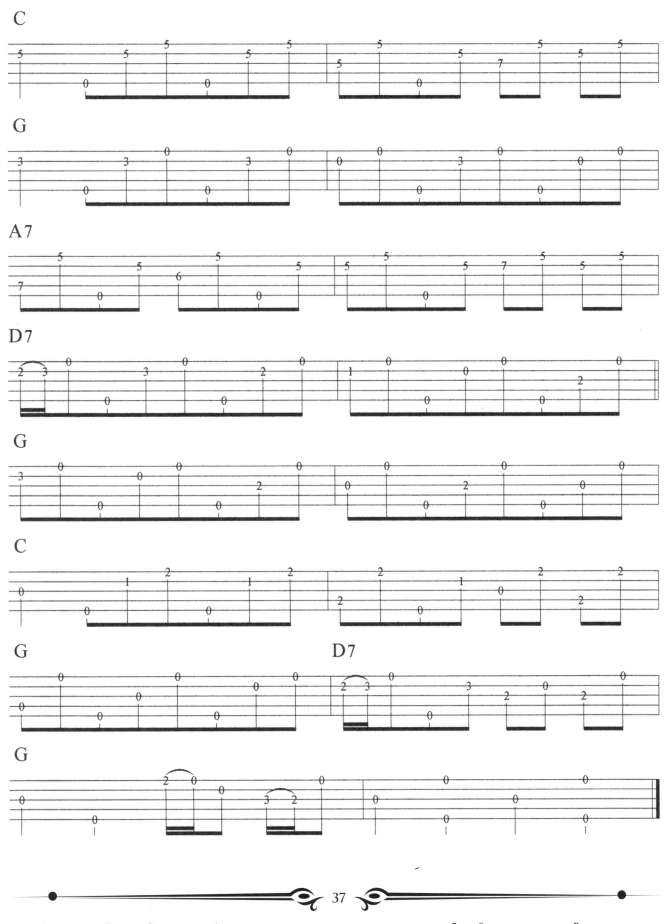

SIDE BY SIDE ARRANGEMENTS FOR 5-STRING BANJO

WHEN YOU AND I WERE YOUNG, MAGGIE

(FRAILING / CLAWHAMMER)

G Tuning: gDGBD

TRADITIONAL

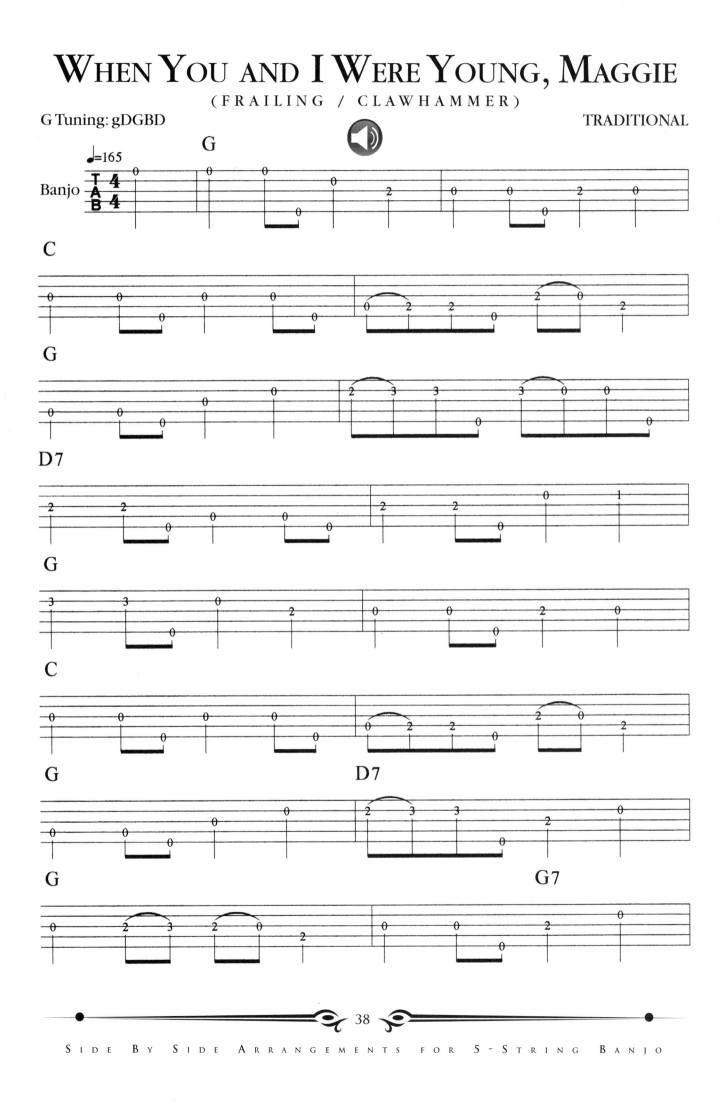

SIDE BY SIDE ARRANGEMENTS FOR 5-STRING BANJO

When You and I Were Young, Maggie
(FRAILING / CLAWHAMMER)

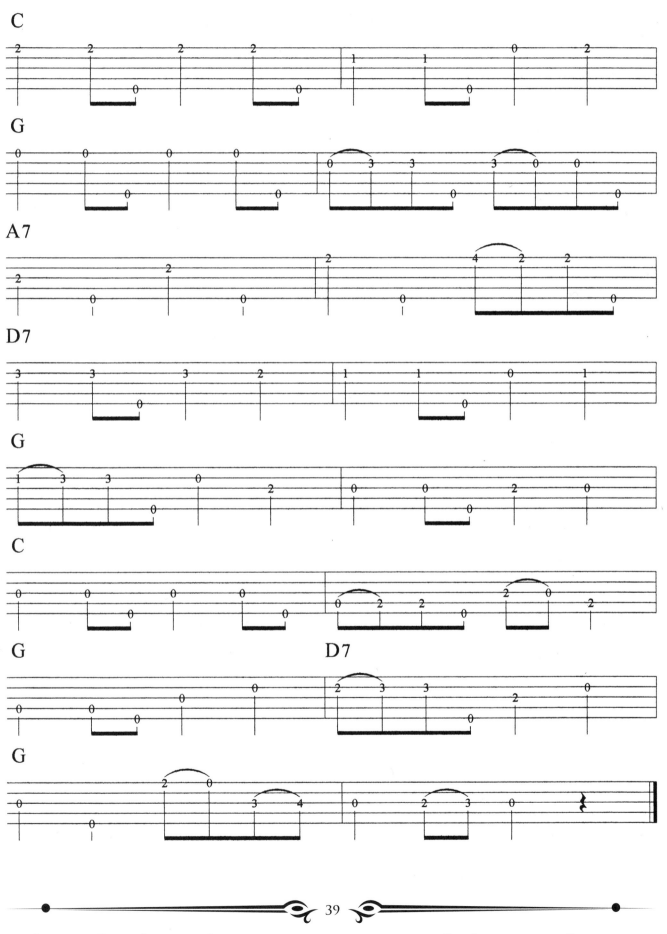

WILDWOOD FLOWER
(3-FINGER STYLE)

Attributed to MAUD IRVING   G Tuning: gDGBD   J.P. WEBSTER

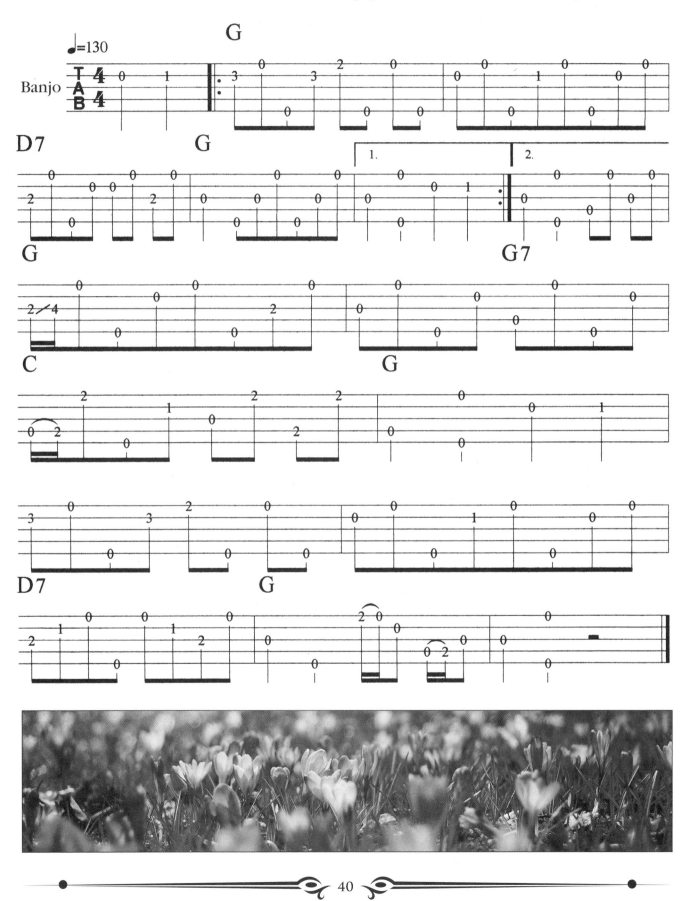

WILDWOOD FLOWER
(FRAILING / CLAWHAMMER)

Attributed to MAUD IRVING   G Tuning: gDGBD   J.P. WEBSTER

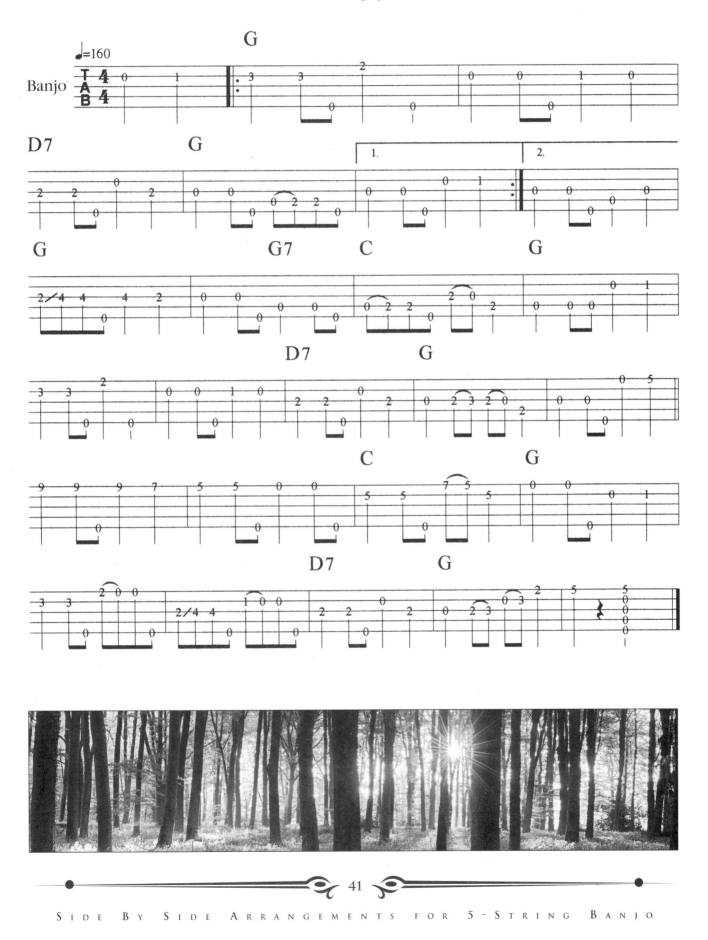

SIDE BY SIDE ARRANGEMENTS FOR 5-STRING BANJO

WILL THE CIRCLE BE UNBROKEN

(3-FINGER STYLE)

ADA HABERSHON   G Tuning: gDGBD   C.H. GABRIEL

WILL THE CIRCLE BE UNBROKEN
(FRAILING / CLAWHAMMER)

ADA HABERSHON   G Tuning: gDGBD   C.H. GABRIEL

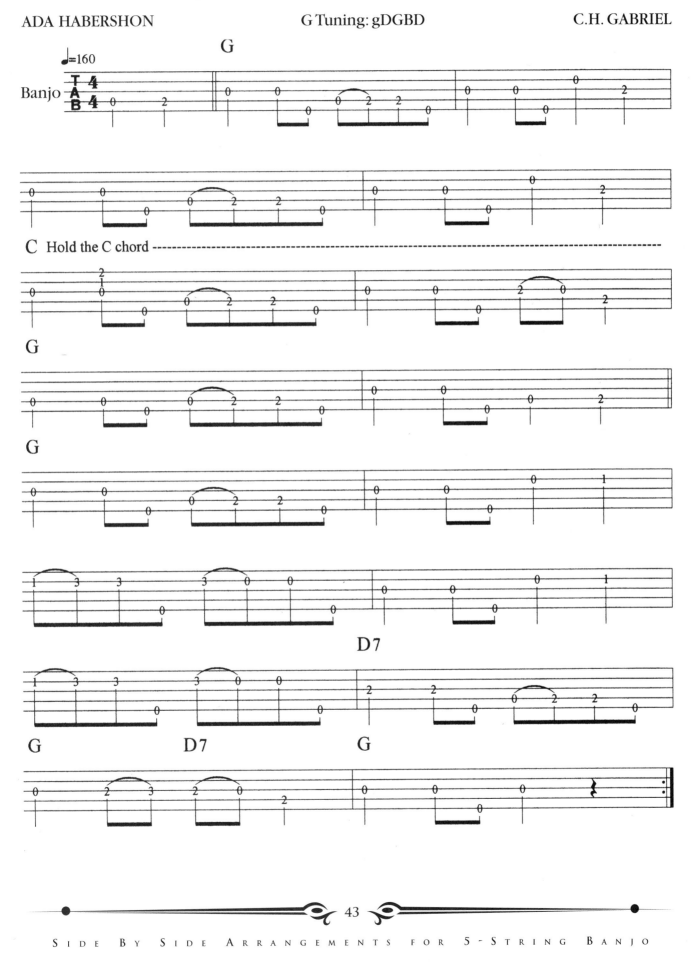

ADDITIONAL SONG LYRICS

DARLIN' COREY

Wake up, wake up, darlin' Corey,
    What makes you sleep so sound?
Revenue Officer, he's a coming,
    Gonna tear your still house down.

The first time I seen darlin' Corey,
    She was standing by the banks of the sea.
She had a pistol tied around her body
    And a banjo on her knee.

The last time I seen darlin' Corey,
    She had a dram glass in her hand.
She was drinking away her troubles,
    Foolin' round with some other man.

Go 'way, go 'way, darlin' Corey,
    Quit hanging around my bed.
Bad liquor's ruining my body,
    Pretty women's gone to my head.

Go dig me a hole in the meadow,
    Go dig me a hole in the ground.
Go dig me a hole in the meadow,
    Gonna lay darlin' Corey down.

Can't you hear them bluebirds a-singing?
    Can't you hear their mournful sound?
They're a-preachin' Corey's funeral
    In some lonesome graveyard ground.

OLD JOE CLARK

VERSES:

Old Joe Clark's a fine old man,
    Tell you the reason why,
Keeps good likker 'round the house,
    Good old rock and rye.

Old Joe Clark's the preacher's son,
    Preached all over the plain,
The only text he ever knew
    Was Hi, Lo, Jack and Game.

Old Joe Clark he had a house
    Fifteen stories high,
And ev'ry story in that house
    Was filled with apple pie.

Old Joe Clark he had a mule,
    Name was Morgan Brown,
And ev'ry tooth in that mule's head
    Was fifteen inches round.

Old Joe Clark he had a cat
    Who'd neither sing nor pray,
Stuck its head in a buttermilk jar
    And washed its sins away.

CHORUS
Round and around, Old Joe Clark,
    Round and around we go,
Round and around, Old Joe Clark,
    And goodbye Betsy Brown.

Fare ye well, Old Joe Clark,
    Fare ye well, I say,
Fare ye well, Old Joe Clark,
    I'm a-goin' away.

WHEN YOU AND I WERE YOUNG, MAGGIE

I wandered today to the hill, Maggie,
    To watch the scene below,
The creek and the creaking old mill, Maggie,
    Where we use to long ago.

The green grove is gone from the hill, Maggie,
    Where first the daisies sprung,
The creaking old mill is still, Maggie,
    Since you and I were young.

They say I am feeble with age, Maggie,
    My steps are much slower than then,
My face is a well written page, Maggie,
    And time all along was the pen.

A city so silent and lone, Maggie,
 Where the young and the gay and the best
In polished white mansions of stone, Maggie,
 Have each found a place of rest.
Is built where the birds used to play, Maggie,
 And join in the songs that were sung,
For we sang as gay as they, Maggie,
 When you and I were young.

They say we are aged and gray, Maggie,
 As sprays by the white breakers flung,
But to me you're as fair as you were, Maggie,
 When you and I were young.

CHORUS
And now we are aged and gray, Maggie,
 And the trials of life nearly done,
Let us sing of the days that are gone, Maggie,
 When you and I were young.

WILDWOOD FLOWER

I'll twine 'mid the ringlets
 Of my raven black hair,
The lillies so pale
 And the roses so fair,
The myrtle so bright
 With an emerald hue,
And the pale aronatus
 With eyes of bright blue.

I'll sing and I'll dance,
 My laugh shall be gay,
I'll cease this wild weeping
 Drive sorrow away,
Though my heart is now breaking,
 He never shall know,
That his name made me tremble
 And my pale cheeks to glow.

I'll think of him never
 I'll be wildly gay,
I'll charm ev'ry heart
 And the crowd I will sway,

I'll live yet to see him
 Regret the dark hour
When he won, then rejected,
 The frail wildwood flower.

He told me he loved me
 And promised to love,
Through ill and misfortune
 All others above,
Another has won him,
 Ah, misery to tell;
He left me in silence
 No word of farewell!

He taught me to love him
 He called me his flower
That blossomed for him
 All the brighter each hour,
But I woke from my dreaming,
 My idol was clay;
My visions of love
 Have all faded away.

WILL THE CIRCLE
BE UNBROKEN

There are loved ones in the glory
 Whose dear forms you often miss.
When you close your earthly story,
 Will you join them in their bliss?

CHORUS
Will the circle be unbroken
 By and by, by and by?
Is a better home awaiting
 In the sky, in the sky?

In the joyous days of childhood
 Oft they told of wondrous love
Pointed to the dying Savior,
 Now they dwell with Him above.
CHORUS

You remember songs of heaven
    Which you sang with childish voice.
Do you love the hymns they taught you
    Or are songs of earth your choice?

The Carter Family recorded a variant version of this song in 1935. Its lyrics are somber depicting a funeral for the singer's mother. The chorus is basically the same, inserting the word "Lord" after the first "By and by" and the first "In the sky."

Here are a few more words to the song I first heard sung and played on the 5-string banjo. You can hear it on the Internet performed by its composer, Sir Harry Lauder, sung with the broad Scottish burr of his dialect.

IT'S NICE TO GET UP IN THE MORNING

O, my brither Jock's a baker,
    And he sleeps along wi' me,
In the winter morn Jock has to rise
    And start his work at three,
Before he gets his troosers on,
    His legs are nearly numb,
So while he's standin' shiverin',
    I lie in bed and hum:

Ah, it's nice to get up in the morning,
    When the sun begins to shine,
At four or five or six o'clock
    In the good old summertime.
But when the snow is snowing
    And it's murky overhead,
Oh, it's nice to get up in the morning,
    But it's nicer to lie in bed.

More Great Books from Dick Sheridan...